Responsive Theming for Drupal

Mike Crittenden

Beijing · Cambridge · Farnham · Köln · Sebastopol · Tokyo

Responsive Theming for Drupal

by Mike Crittenden

Printed in the United States of America.

Published by O'Reilly Media, Inc., 1005 Gravenstein Highway North, Sebastopol, CA 95472.

O'Reilly books may be purchased for educational, business, or sales promotional use. Online editions are also available for most titles (*http://my.safaribooksonline.com*). For more information, contact our corporate/institutional sales department: 800-998-9938 or *corporate@oreilly.com*.

Editors: Meghan Blanchette and Allyson MacDonald	**Cover Designer:** Randy Comer
Production Editor: Nicole Shelby	**Interior Designer:** David Futato
Proofreader: Jasmine Kwityn	**Illustrator:** Rebecca Demarest

February 2014:   First Edition

Revision History for the First Edition:

2014-02-05:   First release

See *http://oreilly.com/catalog/errata.csp?isbn=9781449373313* for release details.

ISBN: 978-1-449-37331-3

[LSI]

Table of Contents

Preface

What You'll Find Here

This book will guide you through the basics of proper Drupal 7 theming. This includes things like:

- An introduction to responsive web design (RWD).
- An introduction to Drupal theming as it relates to RWD.
- A discussion of the "what" and the "why" of Drupal-based themes and subthemes.
- A comparison of a few popular base themes (Zen, Omega, and Aurora).
- Step-by-step instructions for creating custom subthemes based on those base themes.
- Some common gotchas, tips, and tricks for building and theming responsive Drupal sites.
- Pointers to more information and next steps that pick up where this book leaves off.

Throughout the book, we'll use as an example a very fake-sounding online business that sells turnip sauce and desperately needs your help.

Intended Audience

This book makes a few assumptions about the reader:

- You should have at least a very basic understanding of Drupal. If you aren't sure what a "node" is, for example, you'll want to learn a bit more about Drupal before diving into this book.

- You should feel comfortable using the command line to run pre-written commands. You won't need enough command-line know-how to write your own commands or do anything tricky, but you will need to run them and read the output.

- You should know and understand HTML and CSS fairly well. If you aren't sure of the difference between a div and a span or between #header and .header, for example, you'll want to study up a bit on that first.

- You should want to become a better, more efficient, more knowledgeable Drupal themer. If you just want to get a site built and out the door and aren't interested in bettering yourself, this book might offer a bit too much detail.

Conventions Used in This Book

The following typographical conventions are used in this book:

Italic

Indicates new terms, URLs, email addresses, filenames, and file extensions.

`Constant width`

Used for program listings, as well as within paragraphs to refer to program elements such as variable or function names, databases, data types, environment variables, statements, and keywords.

This element signifies a tip or suggestion.

This element signifies a general note.

This element indicates a warning or caution.

Using Code Examples

This book is here to help you get your job done. In general, if example code is offered with this book, you may use it in your programs and documentation. You do not need to contact us for permission unless you're reproducing a significant portion of the code. For example, writing a program that uses several chunks of code from this book does not require permission. Selling or distributing a CD-ROM of examples from O'Reilly books does require permission. Answering a question by citing this book and quoting example code does not require permission. Incorporating a significant amount of example code from this book into your product's documentation does require permission.

We appreciate, but do not require, attribution. An attribution usually includes the title, author, publisher, and ISBN. For example: "*Responsive Theming for Drupal* by Mike Crittenden (O'Reilly). Copyright 2014 Mike Crittenden, 978-1-449-37331-3."

If you feel your use of code examples falls outside fair use or the permission given above, feel free to contact us at *permissions@oreilly.com*.

Safari® Books Online

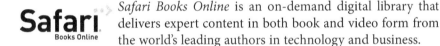 *Safari Books Online* is an on-demand digital library that delivers expert content in both book and video form from the world's leading authors in technology and business.

Technology professionals, software developers, web designers, and business and creative professionals use Safari Books Online as their primary resource for research, problem solving, learning, and certification training.

Safari Books Online offers a range of product mixes and pricing programs for organizations, government agencies, and individuals. Subscribers have access to thousands of books, training videos, and prepublication manuscripts in one fully searchable database from publishers like O'Reilly Media, Prentice Hall Professional, Addison-Wesley Professional, Microsoft Press, Sams, Que, Peachpit Press, Focal Press, Cisco Press, John Wiley & Sons, Syngress, Morgan Kaufmann, IBM Redbooks, Packt, Adobe Press, FT Press, Apress, Manning, New Riders, McGraw-Hill, Jones & Bartlett, Course Technology, and dozens more. For more information about Safari Books Online, please visit us online.

How to Contact Us

Please address comments and questions concerning this book to the publisher:

O'Reilly Media, Inc.
1005 Gravenstein Highway North
Sebastopol, CA 95472

800-998-9938 (in the United States or Canada)
707-829-0515 (international or local)
707-829-0104 (fax)

We have a web page for this book, where we list errata, examples, and any additional information. You can access this page at *http://oreil.ly/responsive-drupal*.

To comment or ask technical questions about this book, send email to *bookques tions@oreilly.com*.

For more information about our books, courses, conferences, and news, see our website at *http://www.oreilly.com*.

Find us on Facebook: *http://facebook.com/oreilly*

Follow us on Twitter: *http://twitter.com/oreillymedia*

Watch us on YouTube: *http://www.youtube.com/oreillymedia*

Acknowledgments

Many thanks to the following technical reviewers:

- Dani Nordin
- Michael Ross
- Rob Decker

And a huge thanks to Mike Granger for the thorough revisions and suggestions.

CHAPTER 1

Responsive Design: A Quick and Dirty Intro

A couple years ago, Riley had a problem. His business—Riley's Terrific Turnip Sauce—was exploding and his phone wouldn't stop ringing with new orders. So Riley did what any ambitious small business owner would do: he took it to the Web. He did a little reading and in a few days' time had set up an online order form so he could take orders 24-7 without ever talking to anyone. This was an overwhelming success.

Fast-forward to now, however, and Riley's tried-and-true order form isn't chugging along like it used to. He's starting to get complaints about it being hard to use on this customer's iPad or not loading right on that customer's smartphone. Riley is once again in a bind and this time he's stumped, so he comes to you for help.

Lucky for you, you've been hearing some shop talk about a thing called responsive design that aims to solve this very problem, but you don't know what the heck it is.

So, What the Heck Is Responsive Design?

In the context of the Web, responsive web design (RWD) is sort of a technical one-size-fits-all paradigm for websites. "All" in this case refers to all resolutions, meaning anything from a tiny Android phone to a 30-inch desktop monitor.

However, unlike that Velcro hat you won in a contest, one size really does fit all with RWD. Rather than just stretching or squishing to fit into the viewing device or browser window as is done in fluid designs, RWD allows you to actually craft different layouts per resolution so that each size gets a truly tailored experience. All that is done with the same code, and without requiring JavaScript (for the most part).

The idea here is to write CSS that only applies to resolutions in a specific range. That way, we can write code that applies only to phones, code that applies only to tablets, and code that applies only to regular desktop/laptop devices.

In responsive design, each resolution range has what's called a "breakpoint" at either end. This is the point where one layout or set of styles transtions to another, often based on device width.

For example, there is often a breakpoint between the layout served to smartphone users and that for tablet users, usually somewhere around 768px device width. You'll often have three breakpoints (smartphone, tablet, and desktop) but you can just as easily have more or less.

A Simple Example

This will make more sense if you look at some code. Like I said, we need a way to make CSS only apply when the site is viewed in a specific resolution, and the way we do that is by using @media queries (referred to as "media queries").

Media queries can do lots of things, but typically you just want to use them to specify a minimum width, a maximum width, or both. Here's what they look like:

```
div.column {
  width: 100px; /* The default, used by desktop browsers. */
}
@media only screen and (max-width: 1024px) {
  div.column {
    width: 20%; /* Override for smaller than desktop browsers (tablets). */
  }
}
@media only screen and (max-width: 767px) {
  div.column {
    width: 100%; /* Override for smaller than tablet browsers (smartphones). */
  }
}
```

Easy, right? Right!

Stop the Scaling!

That code will work fine in desktop browsers, but if you view it on a smartphone it'll still be zoomed out like it is on non-responsive sites. What gives?

To fix this, we have to tell smartphones not to default to zoomed out, and instead just show things at the regular size. To do that, we add this little snippet of code to our markup, in the <head> section:

```
<meta name="viewport" content="width=device-width, initial-scale=1">
```

Now, when we open up the site in a smartphone, it'll be correctly zoomed to normal size and we'll get our beautiful and responsive mobile-friendly styles.

Why Does This Rock?

This is downright life changing for a number of reasons:

- You don't have to snoop user agents on the server side to serve different code.
- You don't have to do any funky JavaScript interaction that alters things after the page has loaded.
- Every visitor gets 100% the same code no matter what device they're using.
- You can reuse (not duplicate) your default code and just override things where needed.
- You can get really specific really easily about which CSS applies to which resolution.
- Built-in browser support for all of the A-level browsers (even in Internet Explorer, starting with version 9).

There are lots of reasons to like RWD, and not very many to dislike it.

Back to Riley

So let's make Riley's simple business site responsive. The site's HTML and default CSS is built for desktop users, so we need to update it to scale down well to tablet visitors and then to smartphone visitors. Luckily, Riley's site is about as simple as they come, and we can get by with just the viewport tag and this super simple CSS:

```
@media only screen and (max-width: 767px) {
  div {
    width: 100%;
    float: none;
  }
}
```

Ta-da! Riley's site is responsive and the users can rejoice! Right? Well, no. The site doesn't break on smartphones, and users can read everything without zooming in and out since everything is just a single column that takes up the full width of the screen.

However, maybe there's more to this picture. In Riley's case, we started with a site built for desktop users and altered it to work for tablet and smartphone users, but is this the right order to follow? Would it make more sense to start with a site built for mobile users and work our way up? Let's talk about that.

Mobile First Versus Desktop First

Whenever you're talking about adapting the user experience to different devices and sizes, you're eventually going to get into a discussion on whether it's better to default to the best possible user experience and then dumb things down on devices that don't support them (i.e., "graceful degradation") or start with the lowest common denominator and add shiny features in for devices that support them (i.e., "progressive enhancement").

You might be asking yourself what the difference is, and if so, you're asking the right question. The difference is subtle, but important.

In graceful degradation, you build the site specifically for users with all the top capabilities and technologies—specifically, desktop users with good, up-to-date browsers. Once that's done, you then selectively remove highly interactive features such as `<canvas>` and high-performance features such as animations for devices that can't handle them and for outdated browsers. You'll also want to adapt the layout as the screen size gets smaller by removing extraneous sections, resizing images, stacking columns on top of each other rather than beside each other, and so on.

In progressive enhancement, you build the site first for mobile users. This means you make the site for users with touch-based devices and a small screen, so all the functionality you provide or the designs you come up with are specifically designed to look good and work well on smartphones. And then, once that's done, you can restyle the design for larger resolutions or add in things that touch-based users would have trouble with.

In this book, I push progressive enhancement because it makes mobile the default, and for good reason.

Mobile Web Users Are A Huge Sector and Growing Fast

There are well over a billion mobile web users worldwide (*http://bit.ly/mobile1design*), and a good portion of those are mobile-only users (meaning they almost never use a non-mobile web browser), including about 25% of mobile web users in the United States. Mobile apps have been downloaded over 10 billion times and about 85% of all newly purchased phones have web browsers included.[1]

This is obviously a huge market, and also one that is steadily increasing. So the logical reaction is to accommodate them.

All that said, why can't we default to desktop and still serve mobile users a good experience? Why should mobile be the first target?

---

1. Source: mobiThinking's compendium of 2013 mobile statistics (*http://bit.ly/2013-mobile-stats*).

The Importance of the First Target

It's important to target mobile first, because mobile users are quickly becoming the most important demographic for the majority of new websites. Targeting them first ensures that they have the best experience possible.

Think about it logically. If you build a site for desktop users, everything else becomes an afterthought by definition. For example, suppose that your desktop design includes a fancy slideshow, a sweet widescreen layout, or some hover effects. When the time comes to make it work for mobile, you'll probably just remove that stuff and replace it with the bare minimum. You might cut out the slideshow or just display all of the items at once. You might stack the widescreen layout with each section on top of the next. You might remove whatever section had the hover effects, if they're not absolutely necessary. In the end, mobile users will probably end up with what is basically the desktop site except with stuff removed or rearranged so that it doesn't break on mobile.

However, if you build with mobile first in mind, you're a lot more likely to take advantage of everything mobile has to offer. Maybe you'll be able to make use of the touchscreen to build a rich touch-based UI. Maybe you'll use the accelerometer for some interactive feature. Maybe you are just more likely to build an awesome design that looks great on small resolutions than if you were just trimming down a desktop design.

How Mobile First Changes Our Example

Let's put this in terms of (very very simple) code. The super simple CSS I created for Riley earlier is a desktop-first example, since the default styles are for desktop users and then we override them for tablet and mobile users. Here's how it looks when you update it to be mobile first:

```
div.column {
  width: 100%; /* The default, used by mobile browsers. */
}
@media only screen and (min-width: 768px) {
  div.column {
    width: 20%; /* Override for larger than mobile browsers (tablets). */
  }
}
@media only screen and (min-width: 1024px) {
  div.column {
    width: 100px; /* Override for larger than tablet browsers (desktops). */
  }
}
```

Can you see the difference? It's all about what gets the default styles, and what gets the overridden styles. Like I said, a subtle difference, but an important one.

Back to Riley (Again)

How could we have altered Riley's site so that it's not only responsive, but also follows the mobile-first methodology? Well, it's a little more complicated given that we were provided with desktop CSS as the default and we need to make mobile CSS the default, thereby providing the desktop CSS in the form of overrides, but as always, it's possible.

Ideally, we'd want to do a from-scratch design for mobile using the basic style guide and branding from the existing site, and then adapt that to the desktop. That may mean a bit of a desktop redesign, but for good reason (as explained earlier).

Now you're familiar with the basics of responsive web design in general, but you probably have no idea how to apply it to Drupal. Don't worry, I didn't forget—after all, that is the point of this book, right? So let's see!

CHAPTER 2

Responsive, Meet Drupal

So this responsive web design stuff is all fine and good, but isn't this book supposed to be about Drupal? Well, you want Drupal, and Drupal you shall have. Let's talk about adding responsiveness to a Drupal 7 theme.

A Bit of A Primer on Drupal Theming

Before we get too deep into the weeds on making Drupal responsive, let's back up a bit and talk about Drupal theming in general to make sure we're all on the same page. To start, you should be familiar with the following terms:

Drush
> Drupal's command-line interface. It gives you commands for doing things like clearing cache, updating modules and themes, running arbitrary PHP within the context of a fully bootstrapped Drupal, syncing databases and files between environments, and much much more. It's basically a must-have for any and all Drupal developers at this point.

Base themes
> Used as the basis for subthemes, these provide a lot of commonly used theming functionality to be inherited, extended, and altered for your use.

Subthemes
> Custom-built themes that inherit from base themes. For example, if you use the Zen base theme, you could build a subtheme that lists Zen as its base theme, telling Drupal to load everything in Zen first and then load everything in your subtheme, some of which might alter or override the Zen defaults.

Moving on from there, you need to understand the basic anatomy of a Drupal theme. There are a few common files you'll find in just about any Drupal theme:

THEMENAME.info

This file contains metadata about your theme, such as its human-readable title, its base theme, and a description. It will also contain Drupal.org-generated version info for any themes downloaded from Drupal.org.

template.php

This file is for preprocess functions. This gives your theme a chance to alter variables after Drupal's backend is done generating them but before they touch the templates. So, for example, if you want to change the way that breadcrumbs are rendered, you would write a `THEMENAME_breadcrumb()` in your theme's *template.php* that gets passed the raw breadcrumb array as a parameter so that you can have full control over how rendering and markup look.

theme-settings.php

This file is built to handle exactly what the name indicates—custom settings for your theme. This gives us the ability to add custom GUI configuration fields to our theme that we can then use in the theme's code. Some base themes take this quite far and provide GUI-based options for layouts, colors, fonts, and more.

tpl.php

These files, sometimes lovingly called "tipplefips," are your templates. Once Drupal sends data to your theme and your theme's *template.php* file has had a chance to alter it, it is finally delivered to individual templates to build the markup. There are many different types of templates, such as the top-level *html.tpl.php* (which contains the `<head>` tag), the *page.tpl.php* (which contains the basic page markup including regions and containers), and individual content templates like *node.tpl.php* or templates for views, panels, or blocks.

With this under our belts, let's get back to our regularly scheduled responsive design discussion.

Adding the Media Queries

As we discussed in Chapter 1, the heart of coding a responsive design is adding media queries to specify which CSS applies to which screen resolutions. At a basic level, this can be done in Drupal just like it would be done outside of Drupal—just put the media queries into the theme's CSS file(s). So, for example, if your theme's main CSS file is at *sites/all/themes/turnip/css/style.css*, all you'd have to do to add responsive styles is to open up that file and drop in a few media queries.

The location in the file tends not to matter, but remember that CSS rules are evaluated from top to bottom. So if the same selector appears in two different places, the CSS rules in the second instance of it will trump the rules in the first instance. For example, if you set the color of paragraphs in one location in a CSS file, and then set it to a different color later in the CSS file, the second rule will win.

There are more advanced ways to do this, which we will discuss later. But there's nothing stopping you from doing it the old-fashioned way, and many people do just that.

Adding the Viewport Meta Tag

Remember from Chapter 1 that there are two pieces to the puzzle: the media queries and the viewport meta tag. The media queries set up the device-specific styles, and the viewport tells mobile devices not to zoom out on the page.

In Drupal, this means we'll have to edit the *html.tpl.php* file in our theme, since that is the file that contains the <head> tag, which is where the viewport meta tag needs to go.

 There are modules to make it a bit more user friendly to add things to your <head> tag, such as Add To Head (*http://bit.ly/addhead*), if you prefer to do it in the GUI. However, be sure to consider whether it's worth adding the bulk of a new module to your site for something as trivial as this.

If you're using a base theme, there's a good chance it already contains an *html.tpl.php* file that you can override in your subtheme. If not, you'll need to copy it from *modules/ system/html.tpl.php* and paste it into your custom theme so that you can override it.

Once you have your own copy in your theme, just edit it and paste the following somewhere in the <head> tag:

```
<meta name="viewport" content="width=device-width, initial-scale=1">
```

Moving on to Base Themes

Although this basic technique works fine, and many people consider this standard practice, there are smarter and fancier ways to go about it with the help of some more advanced base themes.

But first, let's talk about the "why" of base themes. Why is it useful to start from someone else's code when every site has a completely different design? Why not just start your themes from scratch? You can, and you wouldn't be alone in doing so, but you'd be missing out on a lot of useful stuff that base themes provide. They can bring you things like Sass integration, a responsive grid system, some solid default styles for common Drupal elements, and more. Heck, Omega 3.x is even more or less a GUI layout builder.

Sure, you could do all of this yourself in a 100% custom theme, but if you go that route then you have to think about the giant wheel you're wasting your time reinventing.

Why wouldn't you just edit and customize the base theme directly? Why add the extra layer? There are a few reasons:

- You get a clean slate to code on rather than hacking at a preexisting codebase.
- You don't have to fully comprehend any of the base theme's code in order to use it productively, whereas editing it directly requires a deeper level of understanding.
- You can easily apply updates to the base theme without losing your customizations.
- You can have multiple custom themes (whether it's for a multisite setup with a few similar looking sites or a site with different themes for different sections) and have them share the bulk of the heavy lifting in a base theme.

So how do they work? The basic concept of a base theme is one of inheritance. Typically there is a generalized contributed theme used as a framework (or "parent," to continue the inheritance analogy) in addition to a fully custom-built subtheme that overrides, customizes, and makes additions as needed (i.e., the "child" theme or more commonly, the subtheme). A subtheme will inherit 100% of its base theme's code despite not having any of that code within itself, which leaves the themer with a solid starting point and a lot of useful features.

Using a Base Theme

But how does the code look?! It's quite simple. Each theme (whether it's a base theme or a custom subtheme) has a *.info* file that holds metadata about it (name, description, screenshot filename, etc.) and one of the things that you can tell Drupal from within the file is whether or not your custom theme has a base theme, and if so, what it is. A subtheme that inherits from a base theme might sport a *.info* file that looks like this:

```
name = Yourtheme
description = Super-duper awesome thematic action.
version = 1.0
core = 7.x
engine = phptemplate
base theme = zen
stylesheets[all][] = style.css
stylesheets[print][] = print.css
```

See the magic line there? You're right, it's the one that starts with base theme. That alone is all you need to tell Drupal that your custom theme inherits from the "Zen" base theme. If you created a subtheme named "yourtheme" with only one file named *yourtheme.info*, and listed Zen as the base theme in that file, then effectively using "yourtheme" as your site's theme would be exactly the same as just using Zen, because it inherits all of Zen despite the fact that it has no code of its own.

Therefore, all you need to include in your subtheme are customizations, things you're overriding, and additions.

CHAPTER 3

A Short Primer on Sass and Compass

Any conversation about responsive design would be remiss to leave out Sass and Compass. These little guys have slowly crept their way into the Drupal world (thankfully) and we'll go into more detail about that in the next chapter. But first, you (being the astute reader that you are) might find yourself wondering what these words mean. Worry not—it's actually pretty simple:

Sass

> Sass stands for "Syntactically Awesome Stylesheets" and it can be an absolute godsend to anyone who writes a good bit of CSS. It's basically an extension of CSS that adds some great features on top of it and smartly compiles down to regular old CSS so that the browser doesn't know the difference. Some of the nicer parts include nested rules, variables, and mixins, but it brings a lot more than just that to the table.

SCSS

> There are two basic flavors of Sass: Sass (the original) and SCSS (the more CSS-ish alternative). The difference is that SCSS looks and feels a lot like CSS (and any valid CSS is also valid SCSS since it's just a superset of CSS), whereas Sass has a completely different syntax. Sass, like its older brother Haml, uses indentation rather than sticking with curly braces and semicolons to identify blocks. SCSS tends to be more comfortable for those familiar with CSS (which is why the examples in this book use it), but Sass is a little more concise and easily readable once you get used to it.

Compass

> Compass takes things even further. It's a framework built on top of Sass that adds a ton of helpers, pre-build mixins, layout tools, and lots of other cool stuff. It's also a command-line tool (a Ruby gem, specifically) that can watch your Sass files for changes, and automatically compile raw CSS for the browser on the fly.

Installation of Sass/Compass

Before you can do anything fun with Sass/Compass, you'll need to install it to your computer or server first. This should be done wherever you develop; if you develop in a virtual machine (VM), then you'll want to install them there.

The steps required depend on your OS.

Windows users need to first install Ruby using RubyInstaller and can then open up a Ruby command prompt and run:

```
gem install compass
```

OS X users already have Ruby installed, so all you need to do is open up a Terminal window and run:

```
sudo gem install compass
```

Linux users, being naturally intelligent and good looking, know that installation depends on the distribution you're using. Here are Ubuntu instructions if that's your flavor:

```
sudo apt-get install ruby-full rubygems1.8
sudo gem install sass
sudo gem install compass
```

Otherwise, you'll likely want to Google "install compass <distroname>" to find distro-specific instructions.

All that said, it's worth noting that there are some easier-to-use GUI solutions that can automate installation for you as well as provide some nice features such as automatic browser reloading. Here are a few worth checking out:

- Scout: Available for Windows and Mac. Free.
- Compass.app: Available for Windows, Mac, and Linux. Currently costs $10.
- CodeKit: Mac only. Currently costs $28.

Learning Your Way Around Sass/Compass

To start, it's important to get a feel for the cool stuff you can do with Sass. To do this, we will take a chunk of raw CSS and rewrite it with SCSS. Here's our fairly basic-looking CSS:

```
.nav {
  background: #131313;
  border: 1px solid #fafafa;
}

.nav ul {
  list-style-type: none;
```

```
}
.nav ul li {
  margin: 0;
  padding: 0;
  display: inline;
  background: #fafafa;
}

.nav ul li a {
  color: #131313;
}
```

So let's identify some crappy CSS-isms of this code.

- There are hardcoded hex colors repeated in different places.
- Selectors get long and repetitive once you're a few levels deep.
- There are some repeated declarations in both the second and third rules.

Let's convert it to SCSS and see how it can be improved. First, we can rewrite the code, taking advantage of Sass's nesting support:

```
.nav {
  background: #131313;
  border: 1px solid #fafafa;

  ul {
    list-style-type: none;

    li {
      margin: 0;
      padding: 0;
      display: inline;
      background: #fafafa;

      a {
        color: #131313;
      }
    }
  }
}
```

Whew, that really cleaned things up! Now let's see what we can do about those hardcoded colors:

```
$lightgray: #fafafa;
$darkgray: #131313;

.nav {
  background: $darkgray;
  border: 1px solid $lightgray;
```

```scss
ul {
  list-style-type: none;

  li {
    margin: 0;
    padding: 0;
    display: inline;
    background: $lightgray;

    a {
      color: $darkgray;
    }
  }
}
```

Nice! Now we can add those colors to more elements without having to memorize or copy/paste the hex value. And if we need to change one of them sitewide, we're only changing it in one place.

How about taking advantage of some Compass goodies for common tasks, such as forcing the <ul> to be laid out horizontally?

```scss
$lightgray: #fafafa;
$darkgray: #131313;

.nav {
  background: $darkgray;
  border: 1px solid $lightgray;

  ul {
    @include inline-list; /* Yay! See below. */

    li {
      background: $lightgray;

      a {
        color: $darkgray;
      }
    }
  }
}
```

The awesomeness that is `inline-list` is a mixin from Compass that outputs the CSS necessary to make a list appear inline. Specifically, this is what you get:

```scss
@mixin inline-list {
  list-style-type: none;
  &, & li {
    margin: 0px;
    padding: 0px;
    display: inline; } }
```

Feeling the Power

The previous section covered just the tiniest tip of the Sass/Compass iceberg. Let's see some of the other things we can take advantage of.

Let Sass Calculate Your Colors For You

How often do you need to make a link or button a little bit darker when hovered? Instead of opening up a color picker to find a slightly darker color, do something like this:

```
button, .button {
  background: $color-purple;
  &:hover {
    background: darken($color-purple, 20%);
  }
}
```

Or maybe you're looking to build a quick color palette without the manual work? Give this a try:

```
$color-primary: #bada55;
$color-secondary: complement($color-primary);
```

There are lots of useful Sass functions to check out (*http://bit.ly/sass-functs*).

Generate CSS Image Sprites with Compass

Compass can build an image sprite (*http://bit.ly/spriting-comp*) out of a directory of images, generate the SCSS needed to make use of it, and even update things as images in the directory are added/removed/modified.

Is your mind fully blown yet? If not, maybe you'd be interested to know that it can automatically generate `active`, `target`, and `hover` selectors (*http://bit.ly/magic-select*) once you append those words to the images' filenames.

Write Your Own Mixins

Anything from time-savers like combining width and height into the same property to full-blown, awesome-looking speech bubbles can be stuck into a mixin and reused wherever you'd like. Mixins can even take parameters, such as telling it which corner should anchor the arrow on the speech bubble.

Here's one of my favorites. Can you tell what it does?

```
@mixin vendorize($property, $value) {
  -webkit-#{$property}: $value;
  -moz-#{$property}: $value;
  -ms-#{$property}: $value;
  -o-#{$property}: $value;
```

```
    #{$property}: $value;
  }
```

Know Your Plug-ins

If the greatness that Sass and Compass give you just isn't doing it for you, check out the bevy of plug-ins (*http://bit.ly/comp-plugins*) you can make use of to save even more time. Things like grids, buttons, gradients, and slideshows all have some great plug-ins to drop in. But as always, watch out for bloat!

Again, we're really just scratching the surface here. Take a gander at the documentation for Sass (*http://bit.ly/sass-refs*) and the Compass reference (*http://bit.ly/comp-refs*) to see what else you can take advantage of.

Debugging Notes

A slight downside to using Sass is that the CSS that your browser sees isn't CSS that you wrote—it's CSS that was generated from the Sass that you wrote. The reason this is bad is if you inspect an element in your browser's development tools, the line numbers and code are different than in your Sass source.

For example, say you want to reduce the padding on an element. So you open up Firebug or Chrome's developer tools and inspect the element. You can see the CSS selector that targets it and the rule that sets the padding, and you can change it within the dev tools. But that's not the same code that's in your Sass, so you have to figure out where that code is in your source files, or even worse, maybe you're using a mixin or a variable rather than a raw "padding: 10px" property so that's another level.

Luckily, this is no longer an issue due to Sass source maps (*http://bit.ly/source-maps*). Chrome is smart enough to connect to your Sass source files and transparently use them instead of the compiled CSS when inspecting elements.

To enable this killer feature, open up the developer tools (F12 or Tools → Developer Tools) and click the settings cog icon at the bottom right, then turn on "Enable CSS source maps" and "Auto-reload generated CSS" (see Figure 3-1).

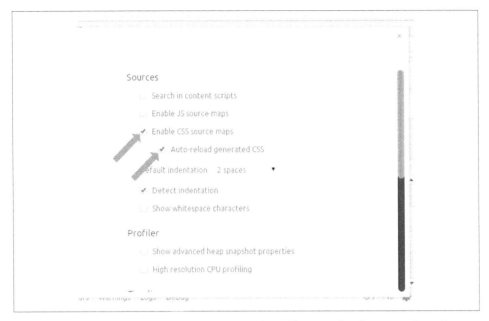

Figure 3-1. Turn on "Enable CSS source maps" and "Auto-reload generated CSS" to enable Sass support

More specifically, what this gives you is the ability to live edit preprocessor source files and view the results without having to leave dev tools or refresh the page. When inspecting any element, the links provided link to the source (in this case, *.scss*) files directly rather than the generated CSS files that the browser is actually using (see Figure 3-2).

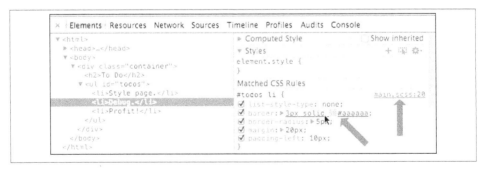

Figure 3-2. Notice that the links to the files are the source .scss files rather than .css

To jump to the source file, you have two options: you can Control + click (or Command + click for Macs) any CSS property name or value to open the source file and jump to the appropriate line for the source of that property; or you can click the provided link to the *.scss* file, which is to the right of the code block (second arrow in Figure 3-1).

Either way will take you directly to the relevant section of the relevant source file, as illustrated in Figure 3-3:

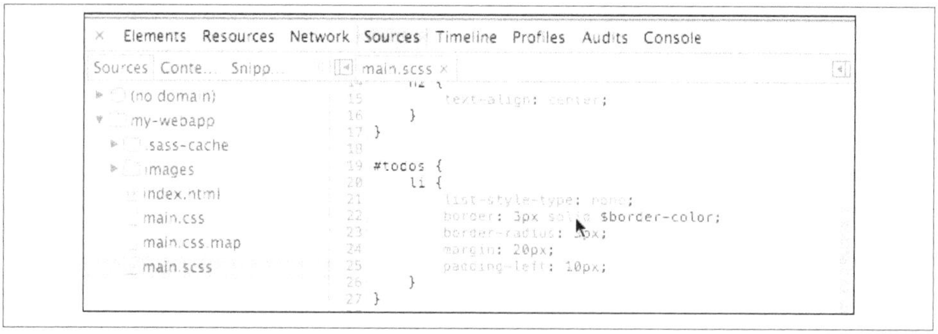

Figure 3-3. You're able to go straight to the Sass source file rather than the CSS file that the browser uses

Moving Right Along

And there we have it—Sass and Compass are really not tough nuts to crack. And once you've cracked them, oh what a world you've found. In the next chapter, we'll apply these technologies to Drupal using the Aurora theme.

CHAPTER 4

Responsive Theming With Aurora

Drupal theming trends have slowly but surely been keeping up with the rest of the frontend world, and one of the leaders of this movement is Sam Richard (aka Snugug) and his Aurora theme. Aurora integrates Sass and Compass into a Drupal theming workflow, and is optimized for mobile-first and responsive design.

Beyond that, it's fairly minimal as base themes go—it basically integrates Sass and Compass into Drupal, sets up a code structure for your Sass, and leaves the rest of the decisions up to you.

In this chapter, we'll put the Sass and Compass intro from the last chapter to good use by walking through the setup and configuration of both the theme itself and a Sass/Compass theming development environment. We'll be touching the command line a bit, but don't fret, it's very simple.

Pros and Cons

Aurora is nice because it's a nimble, lightweight theme with just enough functionality to make you feel like you're not missing out. It sets you up with Sass/Compass and gives you some starter variables and a Sass grid system (Singularity, which we'll get to later) but doesn't hand you a bulky UI for managing layouts or anything like that.

Aurora also gives you the power of the absolute latest and greatest frontend tools. You get Sass/Compass complete with a bunch of useful plug-ins, Bower for package management and Grunt for task management (complete with "Sass compiling, JS hinting, Image Optimization, and app-free live reloading out of the box"), as well as LiveReload and a Ruby gem for creating subthemes. If you haven't heard of some or all of these tools, that's OK—the point is that all of these are becoming the new-school standard practice in the frontend world, and Aurora is one of the very few themes making an effort to keep up with that. It's a lot of fun; it feels young and fresh.

That said, it's worth noting that if you like GUI integration for your base themes (such as a clicky layout/grid builder or a bunch of font/color settings) then you're basically up a creek with Aurora, because that's not how it's done.

It also has a smaller community than Zen or Omega, which can make finding help a bit more difficult. Plus you get the inherent risks of using a bunch of newish technologies like Bower and Grunt—things break, documentation isn't great, whatever.

Getting Started

Since Aurora makes use of Sass and Compass rather than just vanilla CSS, the installation is a little more involved than with other base themes. Let's go ahead and get that out of the way.

Step 1: Install Sass/Compass

First, you'll need to install Sass and Compass as outlined in Chapter 3.

Step 2: Install Aurora

Once you have Sass/Compass installed, you're ready to grab Aurora. First, you'll want to install the "compass-aurora" gem using:

```
gem install compass-aurora
```

Then, just download the Aurora theme from Drupal.org as you would any other theme. You'll also need to install the required Magic (*http://bit.ly/dru-magic*) module for lots of helpers that Aurora integrates, and you might want to install the highly recommend HTML5 Tools (*http://bit.ly/html5-tools*) module as well. If you're curious, you could also check out Aurora's list of recommended modules (*http://bit.ly/list-mods*) that you might find useful.

Step 3: Create Your Custom Subtheme

Once everything is installed, you're ready to generate your custom subtheme. There are three different flavors of subthemes to choose from: Corona, Polaris, and Aurora.

Corona is a subtheme which doesn't give you much predefined organization of your Sass. Rather, it hands you a base folder, a global folder, and a design folder, and leaves the rest up to you. It's the simplest of the three, so it's the one we'll be using in this book's examples. To use Corona, run:

```
compass create YOURTHEMENAME -r aurora --using aurora/corona
```

Polaris makes it easy to write your code in accordance with SMACSS and includes folders/partials laid out according to the guidelines of SMACSS. To base your subtheme on Polaris, run:

```
compass create YOURTHEMENAME -r aurora --using aurora/polaris
```

Aurora is the default. It's based around the idea that you start your theming with a style guide, and as you theme you keep layout and design rules separate. As such, in addition to a global folder, it also includes a style guide folder along with a layout folder and a design folder. To use Aurora, run:

```
compass create YOURTHEMENAME -r aurora --using aurora
```

Once you have your subtheme created, you'll want to install its dependencies. So cd into your subtheme's directory and then run:

```
bundle install
```

Note that if you get Command Not Found errors for bundle, you may have to install it using:

```
gem install bundler
```

Step 4: Configure and Run Compass

At this point, you have everything installed and a custom subtheme set up, so you're ready to roll.

First, you should open up your subtheme's *config.rb* file and take a glance at the default settings to get a feel for the options and see if you'd like to change anything. Particularly, you will likely want to uncomment the following line so that your browser's dev tools can map the generated CSS to the location in the source Sass files:

```
# In development, we can turn on the debug_info
# to use with FireSass or Chrome Web Inspector.
# Uncomment:
# debug = true
```

Once you're happy with that, all you need to do is tell Compass to start watching your Sass files for changes, so it knows when to recompile your CSS. So make sure you're still in your subtheme's directory, and then run:

```
bundle exec compass watch
```

Note that you could technically also just run compass watch but the bundle exec part makes sure that it uses the gem versions specified by Aurora.

Now, any time you make a change to any Sass files in your subtheme, Compass will see that and will instantly regenerate the CSS the browser uses. So by the time you switch to your browser and refresh the page, you should see your newly generated CSS.

Note that you'll probably be running that four-word command every time you start working on your theme and it can get kind of tiresome. You might want to add something like this to your bash or zsh config so you can just type becw instead:

```
alias becw='bundle exec compass watch'
```

Step 5: Perform a Sanity Check

Just to make sure everything's working correctly, you'll want to open up one of your subtheme's Sass files (e.g., *sass/partials/design/_design.scss*) and make an obvious change such as the following:

```
body {
  background: red;
}
```

Then watch the command-line output in the Terminal where Compass is running. You should see it telling you that it detected a change and is rebuilding *style.css*:

```
Change detected at 10:34:47 to: partials/design/_design.scss
overwrite stylesheets/style.css
```

Once that completes, switch to your browser and refresh your page. If your subtheme is set as the default theme and everything went according to plan, you should be presented with a horrible-looking red background. Success! You're ready to work.

Digging Into Aurora

At this point, everything is installed and the groundwork has been laid. So open up your subtheme's directory and start taking a look around to get acquainted with your new best friend!

Aurora's Goodie Bag

Remember that Aurora is basically a simple connector from Sass/Compass to Drupal and it really doesn't provide a ton of functionality outside of that. But it does bring a few goodies that aren't in vanilla Sass/Compass which you should know about:

- Singularity (*http://bit.ly/sass-singularity*) is a Sassy grid system.
- Breakpoint (*http://bit.ly/sass-breakpoint*) makes it simple to write media queries in Sass.
- Color Schemer (*http://bit.ly/sass-color*) is a toolkit for generating color schemes and altering existing colors such as adjusting lightness or tint.

- Sassy Buttons (*http://bit.ly/sassy-buttons*) are beautiful and simple CSS3 buttons created in a few lines of Sass.
- Toolkit (*http://bit.ly/sass-toolkit*) is a Swiss Army knife for progressive enhancement and responsive web design and includes a lot of miscellaneous helpers.
- Compass Normalize (*http://bit.ly/comp-normal*) allows you to use normalize.css (*http://bit.ly/normalcss*) without having to download it separately.

So you have a basic grasp of the hotness that Sass, Compass, and Aurora bring to the table. Now let's dig into the code.

A Primer on Aurora's Sass Structure

Check out the *sass/* directory. Assuming you used the Corona flavor of Aurora, it should look like this:

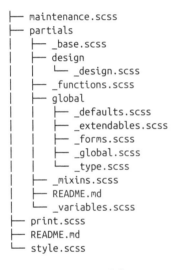

```
├── maintenance.scss
├── partials
│   ├── _base.scss
│   ├── design
│   │   └── _design.scss
│   ├── _functions.scss
│   ├── global
│   │   ├── _defaults.scss
│   │   ├── _extendables.scss
│   │   ├── _forms.scss
│   │   ├── _global.scss
│   │   └── _type.scss
│   ├── _mixins.scss
│   ├── README.md
│   └── _variables.scss
├── print.scss
├── README.md
└── style.scss

3 directories, 15 files
```

Let's go down the line here and dig in deeper to see what each file and directory is used for:

- *maintenance.scss* is used to generate *maintenance.css*, which is specifically for styling the maintenance page. Add custom maintenance page styles here.
- *print.scss* is used to generate *print.css*, which is specifically for styling printed web pages. Add custom print styles here.
- *style.scss* is used to generate style.css which is basically the compilation of all your SCSS into a single file which the browser can see. You shouldn't add any code to this file except perhaps some additional imports if you add new partials.

- *partials/* is where your SCSS is actually going to go. We'll take a deep dive there in a moment.

And if we dig into the *partials/* directory a bit more, we discover:

- *_base.scss* contains imports to partials that need to be included on all three generated stylesheets (i.e., *print.css*, *maintenance.css*, and *style.css*).
- *_functions.scss* can hold all of your custom function partials.
- *_mixins.scss* holds all of your custom mixins.
- *_variables.scss* holds custom variables in addition to some defaults that Aurora gives you. These include colors, font stacks, and breakpoints, among other things.
- *design/* is meant to contain element-specific design styles. I recommend splitting these types of styles into separate files per section, per page, or per feature, so that you're not clumping all non-global design styles into one file.
  — *_design.scss* should be used to include the other (custom-made) partials in the *design/* directory.
- *global/* is where any general styles that should apply to the entire site reside.
  — *_defaults.scss* contains any catchall default styles that don't belong in the other files in this directory.
  — *_extendables.scss* is for any basic global classes you like to create and use such as `.clearfix` or `.nopad`.
  — *_forms.scss* should contain default form styles.
  — *_global.scss* contains no custom styles, and merely imports the other files.
  — *_type.scss* sets default typographical styles.

Getting to Work

Finally! Let's add some pretty! Have you already run the following command to tell Compass to watch for changes to your Sass?

```
bundle exec compass watch
```

Yes? Great! No? Run it now!

By now you should have a basic idea of how to rock your Aurora subtheme since you know the basics of Sass and Compass. So let's work through a real-world example.

Remember Riley and his turnip sauce business? Let's talk our way through rebuilding his (nonexistent) site in Drupal with Aurora.

Let's start with the variables, so open up *sass/partials/_variables.scss*. In our case, we basically only need to store the font stacks and colors we're using. Luckily, Aurora already comes with some nice font stacks:

```
$times-new-roman: "Times New Roman", Times, Georgia, "DejaVu Serif", serif;
$times:           Times, "Times New Roman", Georgia, "DejaVu Serif", serif;
$georgia:         Georgia, "Times New Roman", "DejaVu Serif", serif;
$verdana:         Verdana, Tahoma, "DejaVu Sans", sans-serif;
$tahoma:          Tahoma, Verdana, "DejaVu Sans", sans-serif;
$helvetica:       Helvetica, Arial, "Nimbus Sans L", sans-serif;
$arial:           Arial, Helvetica, "Nimbus Sans L", sans-serif;
```

So all we need to do is tell Aurora that we want to default to the $georgia stack, and we can do that a little farther down by changing the $font-body property to $georgia. While we're at it, let's make sure that forms use a nice Arial-based stack.

```
$font-body: $georgia;
$form-font-family: $arial;
```

So that gets our fonts in order. Now let's add some color. We only need three colors (besides white and black):

- Light gray (#AAA)
- Dark gray (#333)
- Turnip purple (#D900BC)

A few lines below the font variables, we can see some color variables that hold default branding colors for some popular sites (like YouTube and Facebook). We can add our colors there like so:

```
$color-turnip: #D900BC;
$color-lightgray: #AAA;
$color-darkgray: #333;
```

That does it for the variables, so we can move on to some default styles for elements. For example, we have a form, so let's set up some default form styles. Open up *sass/partials/global/_forms.scss* and add some basic input styling:

```
textarea {
  height: 10em;
}
input,
button,
select,
label,
textarea {
  font-family: $form-font-family;
}
label {
  display: block;
```

```scss
    margin-top: 20px;
    font-weight: bold;
    text-transform: uppercase;
  }
  input[type="text"],
  input[type="password"],
  input[type="email"],
  textarea,
  select {
    display: block;
    border: 1px solid $color-turnip;
    font-size: 16px;
    margin-top: 10px;
    padding: 5px;
    &:focus {
      border: 1px solid $black;
    }
  }
```

In a regular site that's a little more involved than Riley's, you'll also want to add some default typography styles to _type.scss, set up some reusable classes in _extendables.scss, and maybe add some global element-specific styles (for things like tables, horizontal rules, or other non-formy and non-typey things) to _defaults.scss.

Now how about some individual site sections, like the header? If you recall, our boring old static CSS for the header looked like this:

```scss
.header {
  background: black;
  width: 100%;
  overflow: hidden;
}
.header h1 {
  margin: 0;
  padding: 0;
  float: left;
  font-size: 30px;
  color: white;
  font-weight: normal;
  margin: 10px;
}
.header ul {
  float: right;
  margin: 17px 10px 10px;
}
.header ul li {
  display: inline;
  padding: 0 10px;
}
.header ul li a {
  color: white;
  text-decoration: none;
```

```
    text-transform: uppercase;
    font-weight: bold;
    font-size: 16px;
    font-family: $form-font-family;
}
.header ul li a:hover {
  color: #D900BC;
}
```

We can clean that up a lot with some help from Sass. Open up *sass/partials/design/
_design.scss* and you'll find yourself staring at an empty file. Rather than adding code
right there, let's split it up a bit. Add the following line to *_design.scss*, which tells it to
include a new header design file:

```
@import 'header';
```

Now you can create a new file at *sass/partials/design/_header.scss*, which looks like this:

```
#header {
  background: $black;
  width: 100%;
  overflow: hidden;
  h2 {
    margin: 0;.
    padding: 0;
    float: left;
    font-size: 30px;
    color: white;
    font-weight: normal;
    margin: 10px;
  }
  ul {
    float: right;
    margin: 17px 10px 10px;
    li {
      display: inline;
      padding: 0 10px;
      a {
        color: $white;
        text-decoration: none;
        text-transform: uppercase;
        font-weight: bold;
        font-size: 16px;
        font-family: $form-font-family;
        &:hover {
          color: $color-turnip;
        }
      }
    }
  }
}
```

Starting to get the idea? From this point, you'll just need to create a new file in */sass/partials/design* for each of your major site sections. In the case of Riley's turnip sauce business, for example, you'd want a *_hero.scss* for the big hero bar under the header, *_footer.scss* for the bottom, *_photos.scss* for the three-column photo display, and *_orderform.scss* for the display of the order form.

 Remember, you don't by any means have to stick with the code structure provided by Aurora. For example, a lot of themers prefer to have layout rules separated from more designey rules, so you could create a *sass/partials/layouts* directory to hold them.

Making It Responsive

Finally, we've landed. Let's take a peek at how to make a responsive theme using Aurora. This is where the theme really shines.

To do this, we'll make use of two things:

- Singularity, the Sassy grid system that Aurora prefers.
- Breakpoint, a mixin that lets you include media queries without breaking a sweat.

Breakpoint is the easiest to understand, so we'll take a look at that first. Here's a familiar looking bit of CSS that we'll start with:

```
.sidebar {
  width: 100%; /* Full width on mobile */
}
@media (min-width : 768px) and (max-width : 1024px) {
  .sidebar {
    width: 400px; /* Fixed width for tablets */
  }
}
@media (min-width : 1025px) {
  .sidebar {
    width: 25%; /* Fluid width for desktop */
  }
}
```

So here we have a basic mobile-first CSS snippet that tells the browser what width the sidebar should be at different resolutions. Specifically, full width on mobile, fixed width on tablets, and fluid width on desktop.

Now, when we convert this to Sass and make use of the Breakpoint mixin, it looks like this:

```
// Set up our variables in _variables.css.
$tablet: 768px 1024px;
$desktop: 1025px;
```

```
// Set up your layout where you like layout rules.
// I prefer separate files under a custom sass/partials/_layout folder.
.sidebar {
  width: 100%;
  @include breakpoint($tablet) {
    width: 400px;
  }
  @include breakpoint($desktop) {
    width: 25%;
  }
}
```

Not only is this a lot cleaner and more easily readable, it's also a lot more maintainable since you're not hardcoding media query resolutions all over the place.

So that handles media queries. Now how about the grid? This is where things get a little interesting.

For example, let's walk through a simple three-column desktop layout on that collapses to two columns on tablets and a single column on mobile.

Here's what it should look like on desktop:

```
===================================================
|  SIDEBAR  |      CONTENT      |  SIDEBAR  |
|           |                   |           |
|           |                   |           |
|           |                   |           |
|           |                   |           |
|           |                   |           |
|           |                   |           |
|           |                   |           |
|           |                   |           |
|           |                   |           |
|           |                   |           |
===================================================
```

And on tablets, we get two columns over one.:

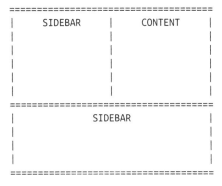

```
=======================================
|    SIDEBAR    |    CONTENT    |
|              |              |
|              |              |
|              |              |
|              |              |
=======================================
|            SIDEBAR            |
|                              |
|                              |
|                              |
=======================================
```

And on mobile, we drop down to a single column layout:

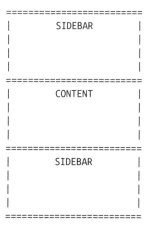

So let's run through setting these up. First, we tell Singularity how many columns we want per layout, like so:

```
$grids: 1  // Mobile
$grids: add-grid(2 at 768px) // Tablet
$grids: add-grid(1 3 1 at 1024px) // Desktop
```

As you can (maybe not) see, the `$grids` property tells Singularity how to set up our grids. If you give it a single number, it just creates that many equal-width columns. If you give it multiple numbers, it creates one column per number, and uses the numbers to determine the relational size between them.

Confused yet? Basically, this just means that if you want a symmetric grid, just tell it how many columns you want. If you want an asymmetric grid, you give it one number per column, where the number is how wide that column is compared to the others. So in our desktop example, we said "1 3 1" which means to create 3 columns, where the first and third are 1/5 of the total width, and the middle one is 3/5 of the total width.

Also of note is the fact that we default to the mobile layout, and then add in grids for tablet and desktop resolutions since we're going with mobile first (like we talked about in Chapter 1). If you want to be super fancy, you can use the `$tablet` and `$desktop` variables created in the Breakpoint section here instead of hardcoding widths.

So now that Singularity knows about our columns, what about the gutters? This part's easy. Just tell it how big the gutter should be in relation to a single column. So if you want the gutter to be 1/4 the size of a single column, you just need to say:

```
$gutters: 1/4;
```

That gives us the foundation for our grid. Now how about actually putting content into it? This is where the "grid-span" mixin comes into play.

Let's say that the markup for our page looks like this:

```
<div class="sidebar-first"></div>
<div class="content"></div>
<div class="sidebar-last"></div>
```

Then to get our desktop layout, all we'd have to do is this:

```
@include breakpoint($desktop) {
  .sidebar-first {
    @include grid-span (1, 1);
  }
  .content {
    @include grid-span (3, 2);
  }
  .sidebar-last {
    @include grid-span (1, 5);
  }
}
```

The first number you pass to grid-span() tells it how many columns you'd like that element to span, and the second number tells it which column you want it to start on. So since we're basically working with a five-column 1-3-1 layout on the desktop, we tell Singularity to let the sidebars span the first and last column, and the content to fill in the space between them.

And of course, since we're interested in responsiveness, we'll need to add rules for tablet and mobile. Here's what the whole shebang looks like when you smush it together:

```
// _variables.scss
$grids: 1  // Mobile
$grids: add-grid(2 at 768px) // Tablet
$grids: add-grid(1 3 1 at 1024px) // Desktop
$gutters: 1/4;

// _layout.scss or something like it
.sidebar-first {
  @include grid-span (1, 1); /* Mobile/Desktop/Tablet */
}
.content {
  @include grid-span (1, 1); /* Mobile */
  @include breakpoint($tablet) {
    @include grid-span (1, 2); /* Tablet */
  }
  @include breakpoint($desktop) {
    @include grid-span (3, 2); /* Desktop */
  }
}
.sidebar-last {
  @include grid-span (1, 1); /* Mobile */
    @include breakpoint($tablet) {
    @include grid-span (2, 1); /* Tablet */
  }
```

```
@include breakpoint($desktop) {
  @include grid-span (1, 5); /* Desktop */
}
}
```

Committin' and Quittin' Time

So you've done a solid day's theming, and you have a newfound love of Sass and Compass. Oh joy! Now you're ready to commit your changes to version control. (You are using version control, right?)

There's a bit of a debate on whether you should commit the compiled CSS to your repository or have it auto-generate on the server instead. Both approaches have their pros and cons.

If you decide to commit your generated CSS, you don't have to worry about adding a server-side build to compile it for you. On the other hand, if you only commit your Sass, you can rest assured that there is one final source of truth in the CSS (i.e., whatever the server itself compiles) rather than whatever each developer's (assuming it's a multiperson dev team) Compass version decides to spit out (thus saving yourself some possible merge conflicts).

Whatever you decide, make sure that your entire team is on the same page about it.

CHAPTER 5

Responsive Theming Using Zen

Zen is perhaps the most well-known Drupal theme, created and maintained by the also well-known John Albin. It's a lightweight, mobile-first responsive base theme with Sass/Compass support and very few opinions about how you should be doing things.

Pros and Cons

At around 111,000 reported installs at the moment, Zen is also almost twice as popular as Omega, which is in the number two spot. This means that you get a big community of users answering questions, writing documentation, and fixing bugs along with some battle hardened code that other base themes can't match.

Why has it been so popular? For one, Zen has been around for a long time. It was first created back in 2006, making it a good bit older than just about all other base themes still being maintained.

It is known as one of the most accessible base themes, and the maintainer has done a lot of work in this regard. Plus, it has RTL support.

Zen has also done a good job of balancing tried-and-true, rock-solid solutions with the cutting edge of frontend development. For example, it picked up Sass/Compass back in 2011, well before most Drupal themers were thinking about it, but it has stayed away from all the fancy plug-ins that might not be widely used or officially supported.

Besides that, it's the brainchild of John Albin, a highly respected member of the Drupal community. You can rest assured that John Albin isn't going to lead you astray.

All that being said, to me the big draw of Zen is that it is extremely non-opinionated (about how code is structured, how layouts are built, or really anything that base themes are often opinionated about) and fairly lightweight as base themes go. Of the three base themes in this book, Zen is definitely the lightest, and a lot of people (myself included) consider that a good thing. It has found the sweet spot between ultra-minimal but useless and feature-rich but bulky.

However, there are some obvious cons here. For one, finding decent documentation on such an old project can be tough because your Google searches will return results from years ago that aren't relevant to current versions.

Perhaps more importantly, it's probably not the most productive theme if you're comfortable with opinionated themes and convention over configuration. For example, it supports whatever grid system you want to throw at it, and sometimes you don't want to have to research a choice yourself—you just want to start building your grid in whatever system it tells you to use.

Getting Started

Let's walk through the steps required to start your theme with Zen as the base. For this section, we'll assume that you're using Drush (*http://drush.ws/*).

Step 1: Install Zen Using Drush

This is done just like any other theme. Just download it from Drupal.org or by running:

```
drush dl zen
```

Then enable it either on the theme's page or by running:

```
drush en zen
```

Finally, you'll want to clear the caches so that Drush can pick up the new Drush command that Zen created:

```
drush cc all
```

Step 2: Create Your Subtheme

Zen comes with some nice Drush integration for creating subthemes, so we're going to take that feature for a spin. Creating a subtheme is easy-peasy with just a single command:

```
drush zen "Your theme name"
```

Replace "Your theme name" with the human-readable name of your theme and Zen will do the rest.

Here I should note that there are a few options you can pass in to customize things a bit. Simply run drush help zen, to see what they are:

```
Options:
  --description    A description of your theme.
  --machine-name   [a-z, 0-9] A machine-readable name for your theme.
```

```
--name        A name for your theme.
--path        The path where your theme will be created.
              Defaults to: sites/all/themes
--without-rtl Remove all RTL stylesheets.
```

So you may end up with something more like this:

```
drush zen "Your theme name"
  --without-rtl
  --machine-name=your_theme
  --description="A custom theme for you"
  --path=sites/yoursite.com/themes
```

Step 3: Set Your Subtheme as the Default Theme

As always, when working with a theme, you have to tell Drupal to start using it. Head on over to the Appearance page (*/admin/appearance*) and click the "Enable and set default" link next to your subtheme.

Now go to the home page of your site. If the content is right but it all looks like a big unstyled mess, then that means you're seeing your subtheme. Yay!

Step 4: Install Sass/Compass

You'll need to install Sass and Compass as outlined in Chapter 3.

Step 5: Install Zen Grids

Now you'll need to install the gem that provides Zen Grids, the sassy grid-system goodness that Zen plays nicely with. To do so, run this command:

```
gem install zen-grids
```

Fire Up Compass

Yay, we're ready to get going! But first we need to tell Compass to start keeping an eye out for file changes so that it can recompile our Sass into regular old CSS for the browser on the fly as changes are made.

To do that, just navigate to your subtheme's directory and run:

```
compass watch
```

As always with Compass, it's a good idea to run a quick sanity check by editing a Sass file to see if Compass detects the change and recompiles the CSS. So go ahead and make an edit to any Sass file and see if you get a message like this:

```
Change detected at 10:34:47 to: some/file/path.scss
overwrite some/css/path.css
```

If so, you're ready to rock. If not, you might want to go through the previous steps one more time to make sure you didn't miss anything.

Getting to Work

You did great at creating that subtheme and installing all the dependencies, so now let's put it to work and start styling your site.

Let's take a little tour of Zen's code. In the root of your subtheme, here's what you'll see:

config.rb
>   The Sass/Compass configuration file

css/
>   Compiled CSS spit out by the Sass compiler

sass/
>   SCSS files; this is your home base

sass-extensions/
>   Used for third-party extensions to Sass, such as Zen Grids (which is the only one there by default); you can also think of this as the *vendor/* directory

images/
>   Theme-related images

js/
>   Theme/presentation-related JavaScript

templates/
>   All *.tpl.php* files go here (node templates, page templates, etc.)

template.php
>   Regular old *template.php* used for preprocess functions

themename.info
>   Regular old *.info* file used to tell Drupal about your theme

So obviously, we will be doing the bulk of our work in the *sass/* diretory since that's where the actual styles go.

The first thing to note is that Zen 5.4 and later tends to encourage the SMACSS ("Scalable and Modular Architecture for CSS") guidelines (*http://smacss.com/*) for categorizing and organizing CSS rules. Explaining the details of SMACSS is outside the scope of this book, but the basic idea is that you organize rules into five buckets:

1. Base — Site defaults that are applied directly to element tags

2. Layout — Used for adjusting placement and flow of page components and areas

3. Module — Used for individual chunks of HTML

4. State — Styles that depend on some dynamic condition (anything that can start with "is," like active, collapsed, published, etc.)

5. Theme — Not used as often and not needed in our case, so we will ignore this one

When we take a look at Zen's Sass files, we can split them up into the SMACSS organization technique, as illustrated in Figure 5-1:

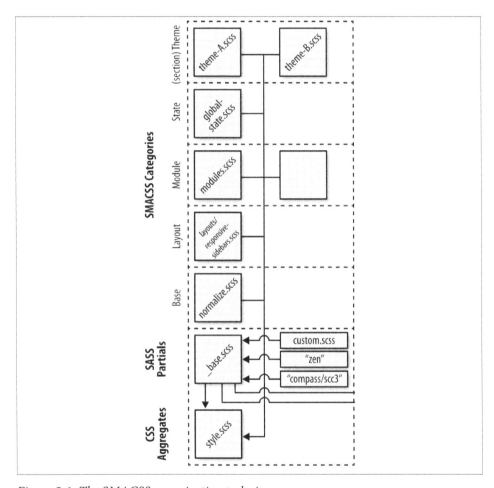

Figure 5-1. The SMACSS organization technique

So at a high level, when theming with Zen 5.4 and later, we want to categorize rules into the Sass files as laid out there.

Working With Zen Grids

Since Zen is a fairly basic implementation of Sass/Compass into Drupal and it doesn't have a lot of theme-specific helpers or anything, there's really not much to talk about that we hadn't already discussed in Chapter 3.

One exception to that is Zen Grids, the grid system built by John Albin and named after Zen itself. Zen Grids is a general purpose Sass grid framework and can be used outside of Drupal just as easily as inside of Drupal.

It's actually strikingly similar to Singularity, as covered in Chapter 4's discussion of Aurora. As an example, let's assume we have some CSS that looks like this, which was taken from Zen Grids' excellent documentation (*http://zengrids.com/help/*):

```
<div class="container">
  <article class="content">
    Tha main content. We like semantic HTML ordering.
  </article>
  <aside class="aside1">
    An aside.
  </aside>
  <aside class="aside2">
    Another aside.
  </aside>
  <footer class="footer1">
    A footer.
  </footer>
  <footer class="footer2">
    Another footer.
  </footer>
</div>
```

Here's what a simple grid might look like, complete with comments about what each line is doing:

```
// Import Zen Grids with this statement.
@import "zen";

// Set the total number of columns in the grid.
$zen-column-count: 7;

// Set the gutter size. A half-gutter is used on each side of each column.
$zen-gutter-width: 10px;

.container {
  // Apply this mixin to the container to initialize the grid on it.
  @include zen-grid-container;
}

.aside1 {
  // Make this grid item span 2 columns and position it in the 1st column.
```

```
    @include zen-grid-item(2, 1);
  }

  .content {
    // Make this grid item span 4 columns and position it in the 3rd column.
    @include zen-grid-item(4, 3);
  }

  .aside2 {
    // Make this grid item span 1 columns and position it in the 7th column.
    @include zen-grid-item(1, 7);
  }

  .footer1 {
    // Apply this mixin to start a new row.
    @include zen-clear();
    // Make this grid item span 3 columns and position it in the 5th column.
    @include zen-grid-item(3, 5);

  }
  .footer2 {
    // Make this grid item span 4 columns and position it in the 1st column.
    // Note that this puts it before footer1 visually despite being after
    // it in the markup.
    @include zen-grid-item(4, 1);
  }
```

That's pretty much all you need to create some advanced grids with Zen Grids. The syntax is about as simple as you're likely to find on a grid system with any amount of flexibility.

And that's more or less a wrap on Zen. It's just a super simple theme that hands you a code structure, some Sass integration, and a grid system, and gets out of your way. Now let's take a look at the opposite end of the spectrum with Omega.

CHAPTER 6

Responsive Theming Using Omega

And then there's Omega (*http://bit.ly/t-omega*). If Zen and Aurora are on the lighter-weight side of base themes, Omega is definitely at the other end. It's a feature-rich, Sass-based theme that can get you there quickly if you stay on the rails.

A Note About Versions

Omega rose to popularity in version 3, which is worlds different than version 4 (the currently recommended version). Here are just a handful of differences, and this barely scratches the surface:

- Version 3 does not include any Sass integration or helpers of any kind, and version 4 highly recommends using Sass.

- Version 3 organized stylesheets primarily by screen width and version 4 gives the user an SMACSS-based code structure by default.

- Version 3 revolves around building layouts and configuring your theme all in the GUI, whereas version 4 does that stuff in code.

- Version 3 relies on the Delta module and the Context module to create customized layouts for pages/sections, and version 4 relies on the power of Sass/Compass and a non-GUI "theme API" (discussed later in this chapter) for creating layouts.

- Version 3 hasn't seen an update for about a year and a half at this point, and version 4 gets frequent updates.

In this book, we will be talking about version 4, but if you're the type of person who finds joy in clicking your way through the theming process, you might find a cozy home in version 3 despite the fact that it is stagnant at this point.

Pros and Cons

Omega 4 has a lot going on, for better or worse. Here are a few randomly picked examples:

- It provides an innovative layout system that lets you define context-sensitive layouts, each with custom regions and CSS.
- It contains a complete rewrite ("cleanup") of all of Drupal core's CSS so that things can be more easily overridden and CSS is more performant and follows best practices.
- It contains a development extension with tools for things like LiveReload integration, a region demo mode, a browser width indicator for responsive theming, and more.

This is just the tip of the iceberg. Omega is big. So, as with most feature-rich tools, it's a trade-off between having a powerful setup out of the box that can make you super productive (good) and feeling bogged down by having to do everything a certain way (bad) or feeling overwhelmed by everything that's going on (also bad).

That said, that's just the nature of having tools that do a lot for you, and which side you take is a personal decision. It says nothing about why Omega specifically is or isn't a good tool.

Moving along, Omega is a very popular theme, coming in second only to Zen in the theme usage ranking. This means that the theme has a lot of eyes on it and a lot of people finding and fixing issues so you don't have to, which is always a good thing. However, the numbers might be a little skewed since a huge chunk of the reported installs are undoubtedly version 3. This means that version 4 might be a good bit less popular than you would think based on the total number alone.

Another downside of the version 3 versus version 4 split is that a lot of the documentation and QA you find on "Omega" is actually for "Omega 3," which can be frustrating for users trying to learn the ropes of version 4. That said, Omega's official documentation for 4.x is quite good.

Finally, it should be noted that version 4 is maintained by Sebastian Siemssen ("fubhy"), who is quite well respected in the community, so that should definitely be a confidence booster to anyone window shopping for base themes.

Getting Started

Using Omega means that you'll be setting up a subtheme of Omega and altering it with the full power of Sass/Compass at your fingertips. In other words, this section is almost identical to the corresponding sections on Aurora ("Getting Started" on page 20) and

Zen ("Getting Started" on page 34). However, there are some tricky differences, as there always tend to be, so let's start at the beginning.

Step 1: Install Sass/Compass

You'll need to install Sass and Compass as outlined in Chapter 3.

Step 2: Create Your Subtheme Using Drush

Omega comes with very useful Drush integration, and creating a subtheme is a great example of this. Omega provides a Drush wizard that guides you through the process of creating a sub-theme, asking questions along the way, until finally exporting a customized and ready-to-hack-on subtheme based on your answers.

To trigger this, run:

```
drush omega-wizard
```

Here are the questions it will run you through, along with some tips for answering:

Please enter the name of the new subtheme [Omega Subtheme]:

Just enter the human-readable name for your theme. Typically this will be based on the name of the website, client, or app itself.

Please enter a machine-readable name for your new theme [omega_subtheme]:

Typically, the default (the value in the square brackets) will be fine. It just converts your subtheme name from the last answer to a machine name by lowercasing and replacing spaces with underscores.

Please choose a base theme for your new theme:

- *[0] : Cancel*
- *[1] : Ohm (Subtheme of Omega) - Omega based demonstration theme. Serves as a best-practice reference for the Omega documentation. Ohm will be constantly updated as best practice evolves so shouldn't be used in production.*
- *[2] : Omega - A powerful HTML5 base theme framework utilizing tools like Sass, Compass, Grunt, Bower, Ruby Version Manager, Bundler and more.*

Just enter 2 here, because you want to use Omega.

Please choose a starterkit for your new theme:

- *[0] : Cancel*
- *[1] : Default: Comes with a well organized Sass setup with heavy use of partials. (Provided by Omega)*

Enter 1 here, obviously.

Please choose a destination type:

- *[0] : Cancel*
- *[1] : Site (e.g. all or example.com)*
- *[2] : Installation profile*
- *[3] : Parent theme*

Usually you'll want to use 1 for this, because it will go in *sites/all/themes* or *sites/site-name.com/themes*, but if you're building a distribution you might want it put directly into an install profile. For this example, let's enter 1.

Please choose a site:

- *[0] : Cancel*
- *[1] : all*

You will get more options here if you have more directories under */sites* than just */sites/all* and */sites/default*, and if you're doing a multisite setup you will definitely want to be mindful of which directory gets the theme. In most cases, though, "all" should be fine, so we'll enter 1.

Do you want to keep the starterkit's readme files? (y/n)

Sure, why not? Let's enter "y."

Do you want to enable your new theme? (y/n):

Yep, might as well. Enter "y."

Do you want to make your new theme the default theme? (y/n):

Again, might as well. Enter "y."

That should be the end of the wizard, so you'll see some output that looks like this, except with your custom theme name on the last line instead of "Theme Name":

```
Beginning to build libraries.make.

selectivizr downloaded from https://github.com/fubhy/selectivizr/archive/master.zip.
html5shiv downloaded from https://github.com/fubhy/html5shiv
  /archive/master.zip.
respond downloaded from https://github.com/fubhy/respond/archive
  /master.zip.
matchmedia downloaded from https://github.com/fubhy/matchmedia/archive/master.zip.
pie downloaded from https://github.com/fubhy/pie/archive/master.zip.
You have successfully created the theme Theme Name (theme_name) in
  sites/all/themes.
```

So now we can head on over to *sites/all/themes/theme_name* (or whatever you named yours) and check out our brand new subtheme.

Drush Integration

When I said that Omega has good Drush integration, I meant it. Here's the full list of Drush commands that come bundled with Omega:

- omega-export (`oexp`): Exports the theme settings of a given theme from the database to the *.info* file.
- omega-guard (`ogrd`): Runs guard for the given theme including Compass and LiveReload by default. We will discuss this in a bit.
- omega-revert (`orev`): Reverts the theme settings of a given theme by deleting them from the database.
- omega-subtheme (`osub`): Creates an Omega subtheme in one step. Requires you to provide options/flags to the command rather than answering questions like the wizard does. Useful for scripting, but not recommended for human usage.
- omega-wizard (`owiz`): Guides you through a wizard for generating a subtheme. This is the proper way for people to create sub-themes.

Also, if you happen to run into a Drush error, you likely need to clear Drush's cache using this command:

```
drush cc drush
```

Taking an Omega Tour

There's a lot going on in the average Omega subtheme directory. Let's take a deep dive. Here's what the tree looks like (given a subtheme with a machine name of "test"):

```
├── bower.json
├── config.rb
├── css
│   ├── test.hacks.css
│   ├── test.no-query.css
│   ├── test.normalize.css
│   └── test.styles.css
├── Gemfile
├── Gruntfile.js
├── Guardfile
├── images
│   └── README.txt
├── js
│   └── test.behaviors.js
├── libraries
│   ├── html5shiv
```

```
│       │   ├── html5shiv.js
│       │   ├── html5shiv.min.js
│       │   ├── html5shiv-printshiv.js
│       │   └── html5shiv-printshiv.min.js
│       ├── matchmedia
│       │   ├── matchmedia.js
│       │   └── matchmedia.min.js
│       ├── pie
│       │   ├── PIE.htc
│       │   └── PIE.js
│       ├── respond
│       │   ├── respond.js
│       │   └── respond.min.js
│       └── selectivizr
│           ├── selectivizr.js
│           └── selectivizr.min.js
├── libraries.make
├── logo.png
├── package.json
├── preprocess
│   ├── page.preprocess.inc
│   └── README.md
├── process
│   ├── page.process.inc
│   └── README.md
├── sass
│   ├── abstractions
│   │   └── README.md
│   ├── base
│   │   ├── _forms.scss
│   │   ├── _lists.scss
│   │   ├── _media.scss
│   │   ├── README.md
│   │   ├── _tables.scss
│   │   └── _typography.scss
│   ├── components
│   │   ├── _navigation.scss
│   │   ├── README.md
│   │   └── _search.scss
│   ├── README.md
│   ├── test.hacks.scss
│   ├── test.no-query.scss
│   ├── test.normalize.scss
│   ├── test.styles.scss
│   └── variables
│       ├── _colors.scss
│       ├── _legacy.scss
│       ├── README.md
│       └── _typography.scss
├── screenshot.png
├── template.php
├── templates
```

```
|     └── README.md
├── test.info
├── theme
|     └── README.md
└── theme-settings.php
```

Pretty intimidating, huh? Well, the good news is that a lot of that can safely be ignored for now, such as some of the configuration files (such as *Gemfile*, *Guardfile*, and *Gruntfile.js*, among others), the compiled CSS, and everything under */libraries*. Here's a trimmed down version of the same thing, with everything we won't need to concern ourselves with removed:

```
├── config.rb
├── images
├── js
|     └── test.behaviors.js
├── preprocess
|     ├── page.preprocess.inc
├── process
|     ├── page.process.inc
├── sass
|     ├── abstractions
|     ├── base
|     |     ├── _forms.scss
|     |     ├── _lists.scss
|     |     ├── _media.scss
|     |     ├── _tables.scss
|     |     └── _typography.scss
|     ├── components
|     |     ├── _navigation.scss
|     |     └── _search.scss
|     ├── test.hacks.scss
|     ├── test.no-query.scss
|     ├── test.normalize.scss
|     ├── test.styles.scss
|     └── variables
|           ├── _colors.scss
|           ├── _legacy.scss
|           └── _typography.scss
├── screenshot.png
├── template.php
├── templates
├── theme
```

That's a much less scary directory tree, no? And most of those subdirectories are pretty self-explanatory. Here's some info on each of them:

```
├── images: theme-specific images such as background images and icons go here.
├── js: theme-specific JS that doesn't make sense to put into a custom module
    goes here
├── preprocess: implementations of preprocess functions go here
├── process: implementations of process functions go here
```

```
├── sass: this holds all of your SCSS files
│       ├── abstractions: Sass mixins, extends and functions for general use.
│       ├── base: styles for basic HTML elements (no classes or IDs) go here.
│       ├── components: i.e., "modules" in SMACCS (as discussed in Chapter 5).
│           More on this below.
│       └── variables: reusable Sass variables such as colors, font-stacks, borders,
│           etc., go here.
├── templates: this holds all of your theme's .tpl.php files.
├── theme: this neat directory holds all of your themename_* functions that
│       would typically go in template.php in other themes. More on this below.
```

Of those, there are perhaps only two that are a bit tricky.

The first, */sass/components*, can be a bit confusing because the typical question is "what is a component?" Luckily, Omega throws us a bone with a *README.md* in that directory that tells us exactly that. In the words of the README, "Components are discrete parts of your page that should sit within the regions of your layouts. You should try to abstract your components as much as possible to promote reuse throughout the theme."

Some common examples in Drupal include things like blocks, specific content types such as viewing an article node (and the individual fields can be subcomponents), individual forms such as the login form and the search form, and specific views.

The second tricky directory is */theme*, which is interesting for two reasons. One, because in just about any other theme, you'd put all that stuff (i.e., *themename**, such as theme name_breadcrumb() and themename_button()) into *template.php*, and two, because it has some neat auto-discovery of filenames based on the functions they contain. The gist is that you can create files in the convention of *<thing-you-are-theming>.theme.inc* which contain themename_thing-you-are-theming_() implementations and it will auto-load them, enabling you to split all that stuff up really cleanly and easily.

For example, if you need to implement themename_breadcrumb(), put it in *theme/breadcrumb.theme.inc*. Note that underscores should become hyphens in filenames, so if you're implementing themename_menu_link() you'll want to put it in *theme/menu-link.theme.inc*.

Responsive Layouts Using Singularity Grids

Omega, like Aurora, encourages using the Singularity grid system. We've already discussed that one (see Chapter 4), so for the sake of completeness, let's talk about a popular alternative by the name of Susy. Susy is a well thought-out grid system which was also used by Aurora before Aurora's own the switch to Singularity.

First of all, you'll need to install Susy, since it doesn't come by default. This is easy enough by just running:

```
gem install susy
```

Along with that, you'll also probably want to add it to your Gemfile.

Secondly, if you're familiar with Sass and getting acquainted with Susy, it can be very helpful to turn on the debugging grid backgrounds like this:

```
@include susy-grid-background
```

You will want to do this under each at-breakpoint to see the different grids take effect.

Now we can build a grid with Susy. We'll start by adding some configuration variables. Create a new file in */sass/variables* called *_layout.scss*, and fill it up with something like this:

```
$total-columns  : 7;
$column-width   : 4em;
$gutter-width   : 1em;
$grid-padding   : $gutter-width;
```

Easy enough, right? We want a seven-column grid where each column is 4ems wide and each gutter is 1em wide, plus we also have 1em of padding.

As for making individual elements conform to the grid, this is also quite simple using the `span-columns()` mixin. The basic syntax for this mixin is as follows:

```
span-columns(<$columns> [<omega> , <$context>, <$padding>, <$from>, <$style>])
```

As for what those placeholders mean:

- `<$columns>`: The number of columns to span.
- `<omega>`: Optional flag to signal the last element in a row.
- `<$context>`: Current nesting context. Default: `$total-columns`.
- `<$padding>`: Optional padding applied inside an individual grid element. Given as a length (in the same units as the grid) or a list of lengths (from-direction to-direction). Default: false.
- `<$from>`: The origin direction of your document flow. Default: `$from-direction`.
- `<$style>`: Optionally return static lengths for grid calculations. Default: `$container-style`.

With that in mind, aligning things into the grid is as simple as adding that mixin to them, like so:

```
#login-form {
  @include span-columns(3, 12);
}
```

Now is a good time to note that Omega also relies heavily on Breakpoint, as does Aurora, so the knowledge from Chapter 4 on targeting specific breakpoints will be true here as well.

Making Use of Custom Layouts

One of Omega's unique features is the ability to create completely custom layouts and tell the site to use them on specific pages.

In Omega 3.x, this was done in the UI, but Omega 4.x forces you to do it in code. To start, you'll need to copy the *layouts/* directory and its contents from the base Omega theme, then paste it into the subtheme you created.

Once inside the subtheme's *layouts/* directory, rename "simple" to whatever you'd like to call your new layout. For example, if you're creating a layout to be used on directory pages, you could call it "directory."

Once that's done, you'll also need to rename the other miscellaneous files inside that directory by replacing "simple" with "directory." This will include three files: *sass/layouts/simple.layout.scss*, *layouts/simple-layout.tpl.php*, and *layouts/simple.layout.inc*.

So rename those files by replacing "simple" with "directory," then make sure to open them up and find/replace all other instances of that word.

Now that that's done, let's talk about what those files do:

LAYOUTNAME.layout.inc
> This file provides some basic info about the layout and lists the regions within it. You can change the regions by adding new ones or removing default ones. As a quick example, if you want to add a new "Featured" region, you'd need to add `regions[featured] = Featured` in this file. Note that if you're adding a new region or changing region names, you must also have a matching region in the *.info* file.

LAYOUTNAME-layout.tpl.php
> This is just a regular old Drupal page template for the layout. This is where the regions listed in *LAYOUTNAME.layout.inc* will actually be outputted, so don't forget to update this file as well if you change your regions in the *.inc* file.

NEWLAYOUT.layout.scss
> This is an SCSS file that generates the CSS which actually builds the layout. It makes use of Susy and Compass, so you should feel right at home.

So now you have the three ingredients you need for your layout: CSS (i.e., Sass), HTML/content (i.e., the *.tpl.php file*), and some metadata (i.e., the *.inc* file). It's a lot like a mini one-template theme if you think about it in that regard.

From here, the process should seem fairly straightforward. Add your Sass rules to the *.layout.scss* file and customize your regions in the *.inc* and the *.tpl.php* files, along with customizing your static markup in the *.tpl.php* file.

The next step in the process is to make the layout actually apply to some page(s) on the site. There are a few ways you can do this. The easiest way is by using the Delta module in combination with Context or Panels to switch layouts based on a GUI-defined set of rules in one of those two modules.

That said, in the spirit of getting our hands dirty and maintaining absolute control, I'd like to focus on the code-based method for applying a layout. That is, rather than using a GUI-based solution like Delta + Context to choose layouts based on certain URLs or triggers, we can swap layouts as needed in code so that we have full control.

Open up your subtheme's *template.php* file and throw in something that looks like this:

```php
function THEMENAME_omega_layout_alter(&$layout) {
  if (arg(0) == 'node' && is_numeric(arg(1))) {
    $nid = arg(1);
    $node = node_load($nid);
    if (isset($node) && $node->type == 'page') {
      $layout = 'LAYOUTNAME';
    }
  }
}
```

You'll want to update the THEMENAME and LAYOUTNAME in that chunk of code, but other than that it should be fairly straightforward. As you can see, that code applies the LAYOUTNAME layout to all Page nodes. You can use the full power of the Drupal API and PHP to select a layout here, so there's really a lot of power. Plus, if you get stuck, you can always fall back on Delta along with Context or Panels to rescue you.

And there we have it. As I mentioned earlier, there's really a lot to Omega and we only touched on a few basics. If you want to see more of what Omega brings to the table, check out Joel Moore's demo video (*http://bit.ly/omega4vid*).

CHAPTER 7

Some Common Gotchas and Tips

It's not all roses and meadows in the world of responsive web design—there are some common issues that throw a wrench into things from time to time, so it's good to be aware of these before they hit so that you can save yourself some frantic Googling.

The basic gist of RWD is that you're trying to reuse as much markup as possible between different resolutions by just styling things differently. However, there are a few cases where that doesn't cut it, and you need to customize things a bit.

Different Resolution-Specific Navigations

Probably the most common area for this to happen is in the site navigation. For example, pretend that Riley's turnip sauce site has a horizontal navigation with hierarchical, multilevel hover-based dropdown menus on desktop resolutions. How would you represent that for mobile resolutions and touch-based interfaces?

For one thing, touch interfaces have no idea when you're hovering or not because there's no mouse pointer to do the hovering. You can always use "touch" to replace "hover" (in fact, browsers on touch interfaces report a hover when you touchdown anyway so that's not hard) but then that presents the problem of "hovering" and "clicking" being the same action. So hover-based dropdown menus in general are out.

So your options are to either display all of the menu options in one giant indented list that takes up three screens worth of scrolling, or figure out some other way to handle the "hover" action.

Select Dropdown as Mobile Navigation

One common method, for better or worse, is to generate a `<select>` dropdown out of the menu items to take the user to the respective menu path when an option is selected.

This brings the advantages of already having good mobile browser integration and already being understandable to the user, as well as not taking up a huge chunk of screen real estate.

The disadvantage is that you're using a form element for something other than its originally intended purpose, and that can feel dirty to you and unexpected to your users at times.

That said, in many cases it's a good choice, and it's fairly easy to implement. You'll be writing a few lines of jQuery that will cycle through your nav links and build a select dropdown out of them. This will be done regardless of screen resolution. Then, you'll use an @media query to show it on mobile and hide the regular nav, and vice versa on desktop.

The jQuery can look something like this, which is taken from from Treehouse's "CSS Tricks page" (*http://bit.ly/convertmenu*):

```
// Create the dropdown base
$("<select />").appendTo("#navigation"); // Use the correct selector

// Create default option "Go to..."
$("<option />", {"selected": "selected", "value" : "", "text" : "Go to..."})
  .appendTo("#navigation select");

// Populate dropdown with menu items
$("#navigation a").each(function() {
  var el = $(this);
  $("<option />", {"value" : el.attr("href"), "text" : el.text()}).
    appendTo("#navigation select");
});

// Make the select dropdown actually work
$("#navigation select").change(function() {
  window.location = $(this).find("option:selected").val();
});
```

That will generate the mobile-specific navigation select dropdown and insert it into the DOM after the desktop-specific navigation element, but that's only half the battle. We also need to make sure the correct navigation is shown on the correct devices. Specifically, we only need the select dropdown to be visible on mobile and we need only the regular nav menu to be shown on non-mobile. So for that, we need this bit of CSS:

```
#navigation select {
  display: none;
}

@media (max-width: 960px) {
  #navigation ul     { display: none; }
  #navigation select { display: inline-block; }
}
```

See how that works? Simple, yeah? Now just make sure you add some styles for the select dropdown so that it will look nice and you're good to go with your mobile-specific unobtrusive nav.

Mobile-Specific Navigation Hidden by Default

Another option is to include a mobile-specific navigation element that starts out hidden. This technique, which was perhaps popularized by Bootstrap (*http://getbootstrap.com*), involves creating a hierarchical nav menu that emulates the format of the desktop drop-down menus, but is hidden by default until the user toggles it.

Often, this involves a little button at the top of the page that looks like three horizontal lines stacked on top of each other. Clicking that button slides down the nav, which is nothing more than a styled unordered list of links.

This way, the user is shown an actual nav (i.e., a list of links) as opposed to a form field (i.e., a select dropdown), but it doesn't take up a huge chunk of space and doesn't involve any funky "hover" interaction. Plus, you can usually use the exact same markup for all resolutions and just do the magic in CSS.

So say the CSS for your desktop hover-based dropdown nav looks something like this:

```
#navigation ul li {
  display: inline-block;
}

#navigation ul li ul {
  display: none;
}

#naviation ul li:hover ul {
  display: block;
}
```

That will obviously hide the submenus by default and show them when you hover their parents. So since we want all of the links to be shown on mobile when the nav is toggled, you'll want to add this:

```
@media (max-width: 960px) {
  #navigation ul li ul {
    display: block;
  }
}
```

And we can't forget about our little navigation toggle button itself. We'll need to always output the markup for that, but hide it on non-mobile, like so:

```
@media (min-width: 961px) {
  #nav-toggle {
    display: none;
  }
}
```

Then, of course you'll want to make the menu hidden by default and only slide down when the user clicks the little button:

```
$('#navigation').hide();
$('#nav-toggle').click(function() {
  $('#navigation').slideToggle();
})
```

And that's that. A mobile- or desktop-ready navigation that is non-obtrusive but fully functional and uses all the same markup.

Dealing with Responsive Images

As any regular mobile web user can tell you, things tend to take a lot longer to load on smartphones. Bandwidth is tougher to come by, and phones are obviously a lot less powerful than their bulkier desktop/laptop cousins. So any way we can make things quicker is a good thing, whether it means less CPU cycles or a smaller download size.

As we all know, images are often a heavy hitter when it comes to download size. Wouldn't it be nice if we could give mobile users smaller images than desktop users? This makes sense for two reasons:

1. Load times decrease substantially
2. Mobile users don't need images to be as big anyway, since smaller files would look just as good on mobile resolutions

It turns out, this isn't very difficult in Drupaltopia. In fact, there is a module that serves that exact purpose. Let's take a look at how that works.

Installation

First, download and install the Picture (*http://bit.ly/dru-pic*) module along with its dependencies, which are the Chaos Tools (*http://bit.ly/chaos-tool*) module and the Breakpoints (*http://bit.ly/dru-break*) module.

Then you'll want to configure your theme by adding breakpoint information into the theme's *.info* file. It will look something like this (make sure to flush the theme cache after changing an *.info* file):

```
breakpoints[mobile] = (min-width: 0px)
breakpoints[narrow] = (min-width: 560px)
breakpoints[wide] = (min-width: 851px)
breakpoints[tv] = only screen and (min-width: 3456px)
```

Once that's done, you can make sure those breakpoints are recognized by going to Configuration → Media → Breakpoints to view them.

 You will need a new breakpoint group for each image style you want to be responsive. For example, if you want the image styles "thumbnail" and "medium" to be responsive, you will probably need to create two breakpoint groups, which you might call "Thumbnail" and "Medium."

After that, you can use the wizard to create the image styles for each breakpoint. Go to Configuration → Media → Breakpoints → "Add responsive style" and fill out the self-explanatory form there.

From there, you can drill down into individual image styles and configure the sizes to, for example, make the mobile styles smaller than the desktop sizes. This is done in the regular Image Styles interface at Configuration → Media → Image Styles.

And finally, once all of that is done, we're ready to map the image styles to the picture options. Head on over to Configuration → Media → Picture to associate your breakpoints with image styles. Now, don't forget that you'll also need to set the display format to "Picture" instead of "Image" in the Display Fields UI for any image fields you want to responsify.

From there, the module should handle the rest. It will output the correct image size and resolution based on the breakpoints you defined, giving your mobile users a much needed bandwidth break and your desktop users the preferred high-resolution versions of images all at once.

Adding a Touch Icon for Mobile/Tablet Touchscreens

If you're going to look good on mobile, you might as well look *good* on mobile, and part of that means providing a slick mobile icon that will show up whenever someone adds your website to their smartphone's home screen.

iPhones and Android phones both look for a link tag with an attribute called "apple-touch-icon" to determine what should show up when adding a website to your home screen. If it's missing, it'll just provide a default icon or use the favicon, which looks terrible. So it's usually a good idea to make sure it's there.

If we were talking about a static site, we'd just want to add this somewhere inside the <head> tag:

```
<link rel="apple-touch-icon" href="/your-custom-icon.png"/>
```

Make sure that whichever image you link to is 60px by 60px, unless you use custom sizes like so:

```
<link rel="apple-touch-icon" href="/your-custom-icon.png">
<link rel="apple-touch-icon" sizes="76x76" href="/your-custom-icon-ipad.png">
<link rel="apple-touch-icon" sizes="120x120"
  href="/your-custom-icon-retina.png">
<link rel="apple-touch-icon" sizes="152x152"
  href="/your-custom-icon-ipad-retina.png">
```

Easy enough, right? Well, Drupal doesn't fight us too much on this one. We'll just need to add that line to our *html.tpl.php* (if your theme doesn't have one, copy and paste the default into your theme). If you open up that file you'll see that it contains a `<head>` tag, so we can just add that line right in there. Of course, you'll want to replace the href with the actual path, whatever that might be.

From there, it's a matter of testing it out by adding a bookmark for your site to your phone's home screen and seeing if the icon shows up. If not, try a Drupal cache flush, and try removing the bookmark on the phone completely (i.e., delete it from the browser app, not just the home screen), then readding it.

Supporting Older Internet Explorer Browsers

The age-old question—what about IE? Which versions of IE should I support? How much effort would it take to get IE8 up to speed? Is IE7 a possibility?

The short answer to this is that you should try your best to convince your client that it's a good idea to drop support for older IE versions (anything under IE9 would be best, if possible). This means that you have to spend less time developing and debugging, and you're able to write a more modern website that isn't bogged down by making things work on old crusty browsers.

However, it also means that you're hanging some users out to dry, so it can sometimes be a tough sell. In most cases, it makes sense to check analytics to see just how many of your users are coming from which browsers and if it's financially viable for the client to lose that user base in the name of easier development and quicker turnaround.

If you do have to support IE8 or earlier, you should first of all note that media queries aren't supported, so you'll have to resort to some sort of polyfill (*http://bit.ly/scott-respond*) to get things up to snuff.

Another option is Breakpoint's No Query Fallbacks (*http://bit.ly/nqf-sass*), which give you a couple options to use besides media queries. Specifically, you can use a separate fallback file that only IE uses, or you can add a class to rules in addition to a media query.

From there, it's just a grind of finding something that looks broken, debugging it using the terrible IE dev tools, doing lots of Googling, and then finding a workaround. This isn't really Drupal specific at all—this is sadly just the lay of the land when it comes to older versions of IE. Drupal can't do much to save you from this.

Styling/Testing Common Drupal Elements

Drupal ships with a lot of default markup and elements, many of which are user facing. Some of these include forms (login, contact, register, etc.), tabs, tables, and lists. It's usually a good idea to test all of these as much as possible to be sure that your theme is bulletproof and can handle whatever a client decides to throw at it.

As always, there's a module for that: Style Guide (*http://bit.ly/dru-style*). It will create a new page that will output a ton of typical Drupal markup and elements. This way, you can get a fairly complete rundown of anything that might appear on other pages all at the same place, so that it's easier to tell at a glance if your theme is handling everything well or not.

If your theme makes all of that stuff look good, then you can feel fairly certain that you're ready for whatever the client is going to throw at you (assuming he or she is only equipped with a WYSIWYG and some node edit forms, as opposed to something crazy like the full Panels interface).

CHAPTER 8

Alternative Options and Next Steps

Congratulations! You have now mastered responsive theming for Drupal, right? Hardly. There's still a lot to learn. The following sections suggest some places you can go from here to continue on your quest.

Study Some More Base Themes

We only talked about three base themes, and all are solid, mature, and popular. But they are by no means the only options. There are many more. Here are a few more you might want to check out:

- AdaptiveTheme (*http://bit.ly/t-adaptive*)
- Bootstrap (*http://bit.ly/t-bootstrap*)
- Foundation (*http://bit.ly/t-foundation*)
- Sasson (*http://bit.ly/t-sasson*)
- Starkish (*http://bit.ly/t-starkish*)
- Basic (*http://bit.ly/t-basic*)
- Skeleton (*http://bit.ly/t-skeleton*)

Even this isn't anywhere near exhaustive. There are dozens, each with their unique pros and cons and differences, and it's definitely worth the effort spent to find one that matches your preferences closely. But to do that, you'll need to understand how they differ.

Learn How to Compare Base Themes

Various base themes can be completely different all around, so it's important to pick one that lines up with your personal preferences. They tend to differ in terms of things like:

- Opinionated versus minimal
- Custom grid versus pre-decided grid
- GUI focused versus code focused
- CSS versus Sass versus LESS

For example, if you prefer minimal base themes that let you handle most/all of the CSS, you might like Starkish or Zen. If you like LESS instead of Sass, check out Bootstrap. If you like building layouts in the GUI, use Omega 3.x. If you like a solid, feature-rich base theme that tries not to do anything crazy, you might feel at home with AdaptiveTheme.

It's all about trying them out and going with what sticks.

Become an Expert on Your Base Theme of Choice

Once you've found your sweet spot, dive in and dive deep. You should know the basics after doing one or two site builds on it, so at that point it's time to move on.

I recommend digging through the issue queues to see if you can answer questions that people ask, especially the ones that you yourself don't already know the answer to, meaning you'll have to do some research.

Or, even better, find bug reports or feature requests and submit a few patches. This is a good way to get yourself acquainted with the internals of what makes the theme tick. After writing a few patches for it, you usually find yourself with a solid understanding of how it's built and how all the pieces fit together.

Or, best of all, apply to be a comaintainer of the base theme to see if you can join its dev team and play a part in the decisions and architecture conversations going forward. This is an awesome way to learn from people who are smarter than you and be a part of something you're passionate about.

Study Up on Some Non-Drupal-Exclusive Responsive Techniques

Obviously, the world of responsive web design is much much bigger than Drupal alone. A lot of the innovation in that world tends to take a while to drip down into Drupal theming, so it's important to stay current with responsive development as a whole.

To start, get acquainted with the heavy hitters. Here's a short list that should get you going.

- "Responsive Web Design" (*http://bit.ly/rwdarticle*) by Ethan Marcotte on *A List Apart*. This is the 2010 article that started it all.

- Modernizr (*http://modernizr.com/*)
- HTML5 Boilerplate (*http://html5boilerplate.com/*)
- Sass (*http://sass-lang.com*)
- Compass (*http://compass-style.org/*)
- Bootstrap (*http://getbootstrap.com/*)
- Foundation (*http://foundation.zurb.com/*)

Once you have worked through that list, the next step is to just stay current with new developments. For that, I recommend subscribing to Responsive Design Weekly (*http://bit.ly/rd-news*), which will give you a good snapshot without burning you out.

Know the Alternatives

Responsive isn't the silver bullet. Different situations call for different solutions, just like any other area of development. If our friend Riley's site was a fancy interactive budget planner with all the bells and whistles rather than a turnip sauce commerce site, then you'd really be shooting yourself in the foot trying to just scale that down for mobile rather than building something specifically for mobile from the ground up. Remember progressive enhancement versus graceful degradation?

Let's take a look at some other options for accommodating mobile and tablet users.

Create a Separate Theme

Use a module like Mobile Theme (*http://bit.ly/mobile-th*) to automatically switch to an alternate theme for mobile users, and you will not be subject to the same confinements that responsive gives you (specifically, the fact that mobile and desktop users have to share the same markup).

There are a few downsides to this. First of all, it means that you more or less have to build two frontends. With two themes comes two sets of block configurations, two sets of templates, two of just about everything. It adds a lot of work.

It also can complicate things if you're going for high performance. It makes configuration of things like Varnish more difficult. This is because it has to make a choice about what to send the user based on the user agent of the user's browser, instead of just sending the same response to every anonymous user who requests that URL.

Serve the Desktop Experience

Mobile browsers are good at displaying desktop-oriented sites by zooming out by default and letting the user swipe around from spot to spot. People are used to this and it's fine in a lot of cases—it's just not going above and beyond like we as web developers love to do.

That said, this is obviously not the optimal solution and should only be used in cases where budget or time absolutely prevents any kind of work on the mobile/tablet front. It makes sites harder to navigate, it makes certain interactions impossible, it leaves lots of users frustrated, and it's just all around a bad thing to do if you can help it.

Provide a Mobile App

In some cases, a mobile browser just isn't going to be able to handle the level of interaction that your site needs. If you have a highly interactive desktop experience that won't translate well to or perform well on a mobile browser, then a mobile app is a good choice. Just use Drupal as the API with the help of the Services (*http://bit.ly/dru-services*) module or the RESTful Web Services (*http://bit.ly/rest-ws*) module and hit that API from your mobile app.

For example, let's say you built an awesome interactive budgeting site that works like a champ on desktop browsers, but the interaction (with sliders and drag/drop and all the goodies) just doesn't work well as a mobile website. It needs to be a native app for users to get the full experience.

The obvious downside is that it forces the user to download and install something (which most users won't do), but in some cases it's just the only possible solution to do what the client needs to do.

Be A Student of the Community

The most important skill to be a smart and efficient learner is teaching yourself how to stand on the shoulders of Drupal giants. Learn to devise better Google searches, learn to ask a well-crafted question on IRC or the issue queues, and above all learn to be humble and accept that you are almost never the smartest person in the room. This is a powerful realization and one that can be very rewarding.

Squeeze all the juice you can out of the amazing Drupal theming community, and there is *a lot* of juice. Just ask Riley!

About the Author

Mike Crittenden has been developing Drupal sites since the Drupal 5 days, and has worn many hats, such as lead developer, themer, and project manager. He prides himself in being just as comfortable with frontend development as he is with custom module development. He's worked with a wide range of clients, from Fortune 500 companies down to brochureware mom-and-pop sites.

Colophon

The animal on the cover of *Responsive Theming for Drupal* is a scissor-tailed Nightjar (*Hydropsalis torquata*). Sometimes called the fork-tailed Nightjar, this South American bird is known for the males' elongated tail feathers, which can grow to be twice the size of their bodies. These brown, white, and black feathers are primarily used as display pieces during the mating season; females have short tails that contain no white. During courtship, the males and females find an open patch of ground, and while the females sit and watch, the males open and close their wings rapidly and jump into the air. This causes the tail feathers to whip and snap around and demonstrates the male's agility and strength.

The range of the scissor-tailed Nightjar extends through many countries in South America, but is most concentrated in Argentina, Brazil, Bolivia, Paraguay, and Peru. They favor forests and woodlands or the *cerrado*, a kind of savannah with dense vegetation that is found in the more southerly parts of South America. Because they have such a large territory and fairly stable population numbers, this species of bird has been designated "Least Concern" by Birdlife International.

Females can grow up to 30cm long and weigh 70g; the males are slightly smaller. With a primary diet of insects, these birds are experts at snatching moths or beetles out of midair, but will also hunt close to the ground for bugs, ants, crickets, or grasshoppers.

Both sexes contribute to raising the young, but Nightjars do not build any form of nest or structure to protect the eggs, so defending them is an important job. The females lay the eggs directly on the ground and sit on them for 15 days. Males will spread their wings and jump at predators to discourage them, but the female and the clutch still remain vulnerable to attacks. After they are born, chicks stay with their parents for several weeks, and then the breeding pair splits up and will find new partners when the next season arrives.

The cover image is from Johnson's *Natural History*. The cover fonts are URW Typewriter and Guardian Sans. The text font is Adobe Minion Pro; the heading font is Adobe Myriad Condensed; and the code font is Dalton Maag's Ubuntu Mono.

Get even more for your money.

Join the O'Reilly Community, and register the O'Reilly books you own. It's free, and you'll get:

- $4.99 ebook upgrade offer
- 40% upgrade offer on O'Reilly print books
- Membership discounts on books and events
- Free lifetime updates to ebooks and videos
- Multiple ebook formats, DRM FREE
- Participation in the O'Reilly community
- Newsletters
- Account management
- 100% Satisfaction Guarantee

Signing up is easy:

1. **Go to: oreilly.com/go/register**
2. **Create an O'Reilly login.**
3. **Provide your address.**
4. **Register your books.**

Note: English-language books only

To order books online:
oreilly.com/store

For questions about products or an order:
orders@oreilly.com

To sign up to get topic-specific email announcements and/or news about upcoming books, conferences, special offers, and new technologies:
elists@oreilly.com

For technical questions about book content:
booktech@oreilly.com

To submit new book proposals to our editors:
proposals@oreilly.com

O'Reilly books are available in multiple DRM-free ebook formats. For more information:
oreilly.com/ebooks

O'REILLY®

Spreading the knowledge of innovators | oreilly.com

Have it your way.

O'Reilly eBooks

 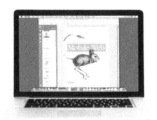  

- Lifetime access to the book when you buy through oreilly.com
- Provided in up to four DRM-free file formats, for use on the devices of your choice: PDF, .epub, Kindle-compatible .mobi, and Android .apk
- Fully searchable, with copy-and-paste and print functionality
- Alerts when files are updated with corrections and additions

oreilly.com/ebooks/

Safari Books Online

- Access the contents and quickly search over 7000 books on technology, business, and certification guides
- Learn from expert video tutorials, and explore thousands of hours of video on technology and design topics
- Download whole books or chapters in PDF format, at no extra cost, to print or read on the go
- Get early access to books as they're being written
- Interact directly with authors of upcoming books
- Save up to 35% on O'Reilly print books

See the complete Safari Library at safari.oreilly.com

O'REILLY®

Spreading the knowledge of innovators.

oreilly.com

Lightning Source UK Ltd.
Milton Keynes UK
UKHW031833250123
415958UK00007B/346